For Maddie and Gracie, who always remind me to keep going.
Thanks for being my rock and my biggest cheerleaders.
Love you to the moon and back!

Introduction to Managing Your Finances: A Roadmap to Success

Welcome to your journey toward financial empowerment! Whether you're stepping into college, starting your career, or navigating the early years of adulthood, understanding how to manage your finances is essential to achieving your goals and building a stable future.

In *Adulting Made Simplish: Finance 101*, you'll find practical advice and strategies for key areas of financial management, such as budgeting, managing debt, saving, and planning for both college and your career. Each chapter is designed to break down complex concepts into simple, actionable steps that will help you gain control of your financial life.

Key Takeaways

At the end of each chapter, you'll find **highlighted key takeaways**. These condensed points serve as quick reminders of the most important lessons. Whether you're reviewing or looking for a refresher, these takeaways will help keep you focused on the next steps in your financial journey.

Helpful Links

Throughout the book, we've included links to useful tools, resources, and additional reading. These links will provide you with deeper insights, help you apply the lessons to your personal finances, and connect you with services like scholarships, budgeting apps, and tax preparation tools. Be sure to take advantage of these resources to stay on track.

Bonus Worksheet Section

Additionally, at the end of each relevant chapter, you'll find a **bonus worksheet section**. These worksheets are designed to help you apply the concepts you've learned directly to your own financial situation. Whether it's tracking your expenses, setting savings goals, or planning your college and career paths, these worksheets will guide you through the process step by step.

Let's Get Started

With a solid understanding of your financial landscape and actionable tools at your fingertips, you're ready to take control of your financial future. Let's dive into the chapters ahead, where we'll cover everything from building a budget to navigating student loans, and from planning for career success to saving for long-term goals.

Your financial journey starts now—let's make it a successful one!

Chapter 1: Money Mindset and Financial Psychology

Transforming Your Money Mindset for Financial Success

"The way you think about money affects the way you spend, save, and invest it." ~ Richard Thaler

When it comes to managing money, your mindset plays a huge role in shaping your financial habits. Your money mindset is the set of beliefs you have about money—whether it's something you view positively or something that causes stress. It impacts how you handle money on a daily basis, your financial goals, and how you approach financial challenges.

Why Money Mindset Matters:

If you grew up with beliefs like "money is hard to come by" or "I'll never be wealthy," these limiting beliefs can hold you back from making smart financial decisions. On the other hand, those with a positive mindset about money tend to make better choices when it comes to saving, budgeting, and investing.

Shifting Your Money Mindset:

1. **Recognize Your Current Money Beliefs:** Take time to reflect on what you were taught about money growing up and how those beliefs affect your actions today. Are you fearful of money, or do you see it as a tool for opportunity and growth?

2. **Start Practicing Gratitude:** Instead of focusing on what you don't have, shift your focus to what you do have. This can help you appreciate the money and opportunities you currently possess and make better financial decisions.

3. **Set Positive Financial Goals:** Approach your finances with a growth mindset. Set goals that are realistic but also stretch you

toward improvement. Celebrate small milestones like paying off a debt or saving a specific amount.

4. **Educate Yourself:** The more you learn about money, the more confident you will feel in your financial decisions. Take advantage of free resources like financial blogs, podcasts, or courses.

Understanding your **money mindset** is the first step in transforming the way you manage your finances. But changing the way you think about money is not always easy, and it requires ongoing effort and learning.

To help you shift your mindset and build a healthier relationship with money, we've compiled a list of resources that can guide you on your journey. These resources are designed to deepen your understanding of financial psychology, provide actionable tips for overcoming limiting beliefs, and support you in developing a positive and empowered approach to managing your finances. Taking these quizzes can provide valuable insights into your financial mindset, empowering you to make more informed and intentional financial choices.

Money Mindset Resources:
1. NerdWallet's Money Personality Quiz: This quiz categorizes your money approach into four types: Money Worship, Money Avoidance, Money Vigilance, and Money Status. Recognizing your type can guide you toward healthier financial habits.
2. Evelyn Lim's Money Mindset Quiz: This assessment helps determine whether your beliefs align with financial abundance or scarcity, offering insights into your financial mindset.
3. Merrill Edge's Money Mindset Quiz: This quiz explores how personal biases influence financial decisions, helping you

understand your financial behaviors.

Merrill Edge

4. <u>Ramsey Solutions' "What Would You Do?" Money Quiz</u>: This interactive quiz presents various financial scenarios to reveal your tendencies as a saver or spender.

Here are a couple of books for you to get a deeper understanding of your money mindset:

1. *<u>The Psychology of Money</u>* (Book by Morgan Housel)
   This book explores the psychological and emotional side of money, offering practical wisdom on how we think about money, the mistakes we make, and the habits we should develop.

2. *<u>You Are a Badass at Making Money (Book by Jen Sincero)</u>*
   A motivational book that helps readers break free of financial fears and embrace a more positive and empowering attitude towards money.

Money Mindset Tip:

Your mindset affects your financial behavior more than you might think. Positive money habits start with believing that you *can* change your financial future.

Quick Exercise:

Think about your earliest memory of money. Was it positive or negative? How do you think that memory influences the way you handle money now?

Budgeting Basics

Understanding the Foundation of Your Financial Future

"Wealth consists not in having great possessions, but in having few wants." ~ Epictetus

Welcome to the Budgeting Basics chapter! Understanding how to budget is one of the most essential skills you can develop as you embark on your financial journey. Think of budgeting as your financial GPS. It's not just about crunching numbers; it's about setting yourself up to live the life you want without stressing about money.

A budget is a powerful tool that helps you control your finances by guiding you toward your goals—whether that's paying off debt, saving for a vacation, or just making sure you don't run out of money before the next payday. In this chapter, we'll break budgeting down into bite-sized, easy-to-understand steps. You'll learn how to track your income and expenses, explore different budgeting methods, and get practical tools to help you along the way.

You may be thinking, "Budgeting sounds restrictive." But here's the thing: it's actually about freedom. When you have a budget, you know exactly where your money is going, which means you can make intentional decisions about how to spend and save. Whether you're saving for a big trip or paying off a credit card, budgeting is your roadmap to making those dreams a reality.

Let's dive into the basics of budgeting and take the first step toward mastering your finances!

Understanding Income and Expenses

"The goal is not to simply make more money. The goal is to make your money do more." ~ Linsey Mills

When you start earning money—whether from a part-time job, allowance, or side hustle—understanding income and expenses is key. These two concepts are the foundation of your budget.

Income is the money you earn. This could be from your paycheck, a weekly allowance, or even a gift on your birthday. It's the cash that you have available to spend, save, or invest. Your income is the starting point of your budget, but it's not unlimited, so it's important to manage it wisely.

Expenses are the things you spend money on. These can be broken down into two categories: **fixed** and **variable**.

- **Fixed expenses** are the things that stay the same each month, like rent or a subscription service.
- **Variable expenses** can change depending on what you're doing, like dining out with friends, buying clothes, or grabbing that late-night snack.

It's important to know how these two work together. If your expenses are greater than your income, it's time to adjust your spending before you start running into trouble. But don't worry—you've got this! Learning how to balance your income with your expenses is the key to financial freedom.

Here's a smart habit: Save a portion of your income *before* spending it. Even if it's just a small amount at first, it helps you prepare for the future and build financial security over time. So, if you can only save $25 a month at first, that's okay—just get started.

Another habit to keep in mind is living within your means. It's tempting to buy everything you want right away, but learning to save and wait for bigger purchases is a key skill. For example, if you want those cool new sneakers, try saving for a few weeks rather than putting them on your credit card.

It's easy to get caught up in impulse spending, especially with little things like snacks or apps. But those little purchases add up fast! Tracking your spending is a great way to see where your money is going, and once you spot the patterns, you can make smarter choices.

Gross Income vs. Net Income

Understanding the difference between **gross income** and **net income** is key to creating an effective budget. It can be a little tricky at first, but once you get the hang of it, you'll be able to make better financial decisions and set more realistic goals.

Gross Income

Gross income is the total amount of money you earn before any deductions are taken out. Think of it as your "pre-tax" income, or what you're technically paid before any bills (like taxes, retirement savings, and health insurance) are taken out of your paycheck.

For example, let's say your job offers you a salary of $3,000 per month. That $3,000 is your gross income. It includes everything you earn—your wages, tips, bonuses, and any additional income sources (like freelance work or side gigs).

Why does gross income matter?

It's important to know your gross income because it gives you a sense of the total amount of money you're earning. But it's not what you actually get to spend, so it's not the number you'll use to build your budget.

Net Income

Net income is the money you actually take home after all deductions, taxes, and withholdings. This is the amount that hits your bank account and is available for you to budget, save, and spend. Think of it as your "take-home pay."

Your **net income** is calculated by subtracting things like:
- **Federal and state taxes**
- **Social Security contributions**
- **Health insurance premiums**
- **Retirement account contributions** (like 401(k) or other employer-sponsored plans)

Let's go back to that $3,000 per month gross income. After taxes, retirement contributions, and insurance are deducted, your net income might be $2,400. That $2,400 is what you'll actually have to work with in your budget.

Why is net income so important?

Net income is the true amount of money you can use in your day-to-day life. It's the money you have available to spend on your needs (like rent, groceries, transportation) and wants (like entertainment, dining out, shopping). For budgeting purposes, your net income is the number you need to focus on.

Why You Need to Focus on Net Income in Your Budget

If you build your budget based on your gross income, you might end up overestimating how much money you actually have to work with. That's why it's crucial to focus on **net income**—that's the number that affects how much you can save, spend, and invest.

Here's how it works: Let's say you want to save 20% of your income. If you budget based on your **gross income**, you'd save $600 ($3,000 x 0.20). But if your **net income** is only $2,400, you'd only be able to save $480 ($2,400 x 0.20).

So, when planning for savings goals, make sure to base it on your **net income**, since that's the amount you'll actually be working with.

Example: Understanding the Impact of Net Income

Let's look at a real-life example:

Sarah's Salary Breakdown

- **Gross Income**: $3,000 per month
- **Deductions**:
  - Federal taxes: $300
  - State taxes: $100
  - Social Security: $186
  - Health insurance: $120
  - 401(k) contribution: $60
- **Net Income**: $3,000 - $300 - $100 - $186 - $120 - $60 = **$2,234**

So, even though Sarah's gross income is $3,000, her take-home pay is only $2,234. That's the amount she has to work with when creating her budget, paying bills, and saving.

What You Can Do With This Information

Knowing your net income is crucial because it gives you a clear picture of your finances. Once you understand what you're really working with, you can make smarter decisions about your spending and saving. Here's what you can do next:

- **Use your net income to set realistic savings goals.** Start by saving a percentage of your net income each month, like 10% or 20%, and gradually increase it as your income grows.
- **Track your spending.** Your expenses should be based on your net income, so make sure your budget reflects what you actually have available. It can be easy to feel like you have more money than you do if you're only looking at your gross income.
- **Plan for the future.** Understanding your net income allows you to plan for things like emergency savings, future big purchases, and even retirement.

By focusing on **net income**, you'll have a more accurate view of what's coming in and going out of your pocket. This is a crucial step to ensuring that your budget is realistic and sustainable in the long run.

Budgeting Basics

"The budget is not just a collection of numbers, but an expression of our values and aspirations." ~ Jack Lew

So, what is budgeting? At its core, budgeting is about planning how you'll spend and save your money. It's about deciding where your money goes each month so you can prioritize your spending and save for the things that matter most to you.

Why Budget?

There are many reasons to budget:

- **Control Your Finances**: A budget helps you get a clear picture of where your money is going so you can make better decisions.
- **Achieve Your Goals**: Whether it's saving for a vacation or paying off debt, a budget helps you put aside money for your financial goals.
- **Prevent Debt**: A budget keeps you from overspending, reducing the risk of falling into debt.

How to Track Your Income and Expenses

The first step in creating your budget is to track where your money is going. Here's how to get started:

1. **List Your Income**: Write down every source of income you receive each month (salary, side jobs, allowances).
2. **Record Your Expenses**: Track everything you spend—be honest about even the small stuff, like coffee runs and snacks. You can break these into two categories:
   - **Fixed Expenses** (rent, utilities, subscriptions)

- ○ **Variable Expenses** (groceries, entertainment, transportation)

Creating Your Budget

Now that you know your income and expenses, it's time to create your budget. Follow these steps:

1. **Estimate Monthly Bills**: Look at your bills from the previous months to get a good idea of your fixed expenses.
2. **Add Variable Expenses**: Track your variable expenses over a month and use that to estimate how much you typically spend.
3. **Set Financial Goals**: Decide how much you want to save each month. Aim to save at least 10% of your income.
4. **Create Your Budget**: Use a budget template (linked at the end of this chapter) to organize your income, expenses, and savings goals.

Reflect on Your Spending

After setting up your budget, take some time each month to review it and adjust as needed. Ask yourself:

- Did I stick to my savings goals?
- Where did I overspend?
- What expenses can I cut back on to reach my goals faster?

By regularly reviewing and adjusting your budget, you'll keep yourself on track to meet your financial goals.

Real-Life Example: Budgeting in Action

Sarah's Vacation Savings

Before budgeting, Sarah loved to travel, but she often found herself short on cash by the end of the month due to her spending habits. Dining out, shopping, and small impulse buys left her without the savings she needed for her dream vacation to Hawaii.

After she started budgeting, Sarah tracked her income and expenses and set a goal to save $200 each month for her trip. By cutting back on unnecessary spending, like dining out and impulse shopping, she saved $1,200 in six months and booked her trip to Hawaii. Budgeting made it possible for Sarah to reach her goals while staying financially stable.

Mike's Debt Dilemma

Mike had just graduated from college and was struggling with credit card debt. After learning about budgeting, he realized he could allocate an extra $150 a month toward paying off his debts. By sticking to his budget, Mike not only paid off his credit card debt but also started improving his credit score, giving him more financial freedom in the future.

Key Takeaways:

- **Budgeting is essential** for taking control of your finances and achieving your goals. It's not about restrictions, but about making intentional choices.
- **Income vs. Expenses**: Understand your income (the money coming in) and your expenses (the money going out) to create a realistic budget.

- **Fixed vs. Variable Expenses**: Separate your expenses into fixed (e.g., rent) and variable (e.g., dining out) to track where your money is going.
- **The 50/30/20 Rule**: A simple guideline for allocating your income: 50% for needs, 30% for wants, and 20% for savings or debt repayment.
- **Tracking and Adjusting**: Regularly review your budget to ensure it reflects your financial goals and make adjustments as needed.

Now that you have a better understanding of how your mindset shapes your financial decisions, it's time to put that knowledge into action. In this next chapter, we'll dive into **budgeting**, a crucial tool for managing your money effectively. A positive mindset makes it easier to embrace budgeting as a means of achieving your financial goals, and we'll guide you step-by-step through the process of creating a budget that works for you. Whether you're saving for a big purchase or simply trying to get a handle on your spending, a good budget is the foundation of financial success.

Budgeting Tip:
A budget isn't about limiting your fun—it's about making sure your money goes where it matters most, so you have more freedom in the long run.

Tip for Success:
Try the "50/30/20 rule" for budgeting: 50% for needs, 30% for wants, and 20% for savings and debt. It's a simple way to stay on track!

Chapter 2: Savings Basics
The Power of Saving: Why It's Important

"Do not save what is left after spending, but spend what is left after saving." ~ Warren Buffett

Saving money may seem like a daunting task, especially when you're juggling expenses like rent, groceries, and entertainment. But here's the truth: Saving doesn't have to be complicated or stressful. In fact, it's one of the most empowering things you can do for your financial future.

In this chapter, we'll dive into the basics of saving—why it's essential, how to start even when money feels tight, and ways to make saving feel more like second nature. The key is to make saving a priority, no matter how small your contributions seem at first. Every little bit adds up, and over time, you'll build a financial cushion that will give you more control and peace of mind.

Start Small, Think Big

When you think about savings, it can be easy to get discouraged. "How can I save when I barely have enough for my bills?" you might ask. The key is to start small, even if it's just a few dollars here and there. The goal isn't to save huge amounts right away, but to develop the habit of saving consistently.

Imagine this: You decide to save $25 a month. While that might not feel like a lot at first, after a year, you've saved $300. That's money that can cover an emergency expense, help you reach a goal, or serve as a foundation for bigger savings.

Here's how you can start:

- **Set small, achievable goals.** Start by saving a little each month, even if it's just $10 or $20. The important thing is getting into the habit.
- **Be consistent.** The power of saving comes from consistency. You don't need to save a ton each month, just make it a regular part of your routine.

Building an Emergency Fund

One of the first savings goals you should work toward is building an **emergency fund**. Life is unpredictable, and having a financial safety net can make all the difference when the unexpected happens—like a car repair, medical bills, or even job loss.

How much should you save?

A good goal is to save enough to cover **three to six months** of living expenses. That might sound like a lot, but don't worry! You don't have to reach that goal all at once. Start by saving a small amount each month, and over time, it will grow.

Here's how you can start:

1. **Track your expenses.** Knowing how much you spend each month is essential for figuring out how much you need in your emergency fund. (The Expense Tracker Worksheet can help you here!)
2. **Save a portion of your income.** Aim to set aside at least 10% of your income each month. You can even start with 5% and work your way up as you get more comfortable.

3. **Automate your savings.** If you can, set up automatic transfers to your emergency fund. This way, you won't have to think about it—money will be saved for you without any extra effort.

Setting Specific Savings Goals

Saving for the unexpected is great, but having specific goals can make saving feel even more motivating. Whether it's a vacation, a down payment on a car, or saving for a big purchase, having a clear goal will help you stay on track and give you something to look forward to.

How to set and achieve your savings goals:

- **Be specific.** Instead of just saying, "I want to save money," make a specific goal. For example, "I want to save $500 for a vacation by the end of the year." The clearer your goal, the easier it will be to stay focused.
- **Break it down.** If your goal is $500, divide that by 12 months. That's about $42 per month. Now, your goal is more manageable.
- **Track your progress.** Use the **Budget Tracker** and **Savings Goal Worksheet** to see how far you've come. Celebrate your progress along the way, even if it's just a small step.

Where to Keep Your Savings: Choosing the Right Account

Now that you've committed to saving, the next step is deciding where to keep your savings. It's tempting to just stash money under your mattress (no judgment here!), but a savings account at a bank or credit union will help your money grow and stay safe.

Types of Savings Accounts:

1. **High-yield savings account**: These accounts earn a higher interest rate than regular savings accounts, helping your money

grow faster. Look for one with no fees and easy access to your funds.

2. **Emergency savings account**: It's a good idea to keep your emergency fund in a separate account. This makes it easier to keep your savings for emergencies and not accidentally dip into it for non-emergencies.

3. **Automatic savings accounts**: Some banks offer savings accounts where a portion of your paycheck is automatically transferred. This is an easy way to save without even thinking about it.

Saving for Retirement: The Sooner, the Better

It may seem like retirement is a lifetime away, but starting early can make a huge difference. The earlier you start saving for retirement, the more time your money has to grow. Thanks to compound interest, even small contributions can grow significantly over time.

How to get started:

- **401(k) or IRA:** If your employer offers a **401(k)** with a match, try to contribute at least enough to get the match. This is essentially free money! If your employer doesn't offer a 401(k), consider opening an **IRA** (Individual Retirement Account) to start saving for your future.

- **Start with small contributions.** Even if you can only save $25 or $50 a month, start now. As your income grows, increase your contributions.

Making Saving a Habit

The best way to build your savings is by making it a habit. The more consistent you are, the easier it becomes. Here are a few tips for making saving part of your routine:

- **Set up automatic transfers.** Treat savings like a bill—money automatically gets transferred from your checking account to your savings account as soon as you get paid.
- **Save first, spend second.** Pay yourself first by putting money into your savings before you pay bills or spend on wants.
- **Cut back on non-essentials.** Look for small ways to save. Do you really need that daily coffee? Or can you skip a few takeout meals? Every little bit helps!

Key Takeaways:
- **Start small**: Begin saving with whatever you can afford, even if it's just a few dollars a week.
- **Build an emergency fund**: Aim to save 3-6 months' worth of expenses for unexpected situations.
- **Set specific goals**: Having clear savings goals makes it easier to stay motivated.
- **Automate your savings**: Set up automatic transfers so saving becomes a habit.
- **Save for retirement**: Start early, even with small amounts, to take advantage of compound interest.

Next Steps

Now that you understand the basics of saving, it's time to take action! Use the **Savings Goal Worksheet** to track your progress and set clear, achievable goals. In the next chapter, we'll dive into **Debt Management** and discuss how to manage debt effectively without sacrificing your financial well-being.

How to Build an Emergency Fund: A Crucial Step Toward Financial

Security

One of the most important financial goals you can set is to build an **emergency fund**. Think of this fund as your safety net. Life has a way of throwing unexpected expenses your way, and an emergency fund will help you navigate those situations without stressing over how to pay for them.

What is an Emergency Fund?

An emergency fund is money you set aside specifically for unexpected expenses. These expenses could be anything from a car repair, a medical bill, or even losing your job unexpectedly. The idea is that when something urgent happens, you'll have money available to deal with it without resorting to credit cards or loans, which can put you further into debt.

How Much Should You Save?

A common rule of thumb is to save between **three to six months' worth of living expenses** in your emergency fund. But don't let that number overwhelm you. You don't have to save it all at once.

- **Start small**: If the idea of saving 3-6 months of expenses feels like too much, don't stress. Start with a smaller goal, like saving $500 or $1,000. That's a great buffer for smaller emergencies like a car repair or unexpected medical bill.
- **Build over time**: As you become more comfortable with saving, gradually increase your emergency fund until you reach that three-to-six-month target.

The key is to get started, and as your income grows, you can gradually build a more robust safety net.

Where Should You Keep Your Emergency Fund?

While you might be tempted to keep your emergency fund in a regular checking account, it's best to keep it somewhere that's safe and earns some interest, but still easily accessible when you need it.

- **High-Yield Savings Account**: This is a great option for your emergency fund. It allows your money to grow through interest, while still being liquid (easy to access).
- **Money Market Account**: Some money market accounts offer higher interest rates and are still easily accessible.
- **Avoid Investing**: Keep in mind that your emergency fund should be for emergencies only. Avoid putting it into risky investments (like stocks or crypto) where you could lose the money when you need it most.

When to Use Your Emergency Fund

This money should only be used for **true emergencies**—things like:

- Medical emergencies or medical bills
- Car repairs or essential home repairs (like plumbing or heating issues)
- Job loss or unexpected loss of income
- Unexpected travel costs (like for a family emergency)

An emergency fund isn't meant for things like vacations, shopping sprees, or big lifestyle upgrades. Keeping this money for only emergencies will ensure it's there when you truly need it.

How to Build Your Emergency Fund

Building your emergency fund requires consistency, but it doesn't have to be overwhelming.

Here's how you can break it down into manageable steps:

1. **Set a monthly savings goal**: Start by deciding how much you can afford to save each month. Even if it's just $25, that's progress. The important thing is consistency.

2. **Track your progress**: Use your **Savings Goal Worksheet** to keep track of how much you've saved. Seeing your progress will motivate you to keep going.

3. **Automate your savings**: Set up an automatic transfer from your checking account to your emergency fund savings account. You can automate this transfer on payday, so you won't even have to think about it.

4. **Cut back on non-essentials**: Look for small, easy ways to free up some cash. Maybe you skip a few coffees, pack lunch a few days a week, or cancel subscriptions you're not using. The money you save can go directly into your emergency fund.

Emergency Fund Tips:

- **Start with a goal that feels achievable**: Maybe aim to save $500 in the next 6 months. Once you've reached that goal, you can aim for a higher target. Breaking it down into smaller steps will make it feel less overwhelming.

- **Don't dip into it for non-emergencies**: When you see your emergency fund growing, it might be tempting to treat it like "extra" cash for things like new clothes or entertainment. Stick to the purpose: only use it for emergencies.

- **Replenish it after use**: If you have to use your emergency fund for something, make it a priority to rebuild it as soon as possible. Life happens, but your emergency fund is there to help you bounce back.

The Peace of Mind That Comes with an Emergency Fund

The true benefit of having an emergency fund is the peace of mind that comes with knowing you're prepared for the unexpected. Whether it's a surprise medical expense, a car breakdown, or job loss, you'll have the financial cushion to manage it without panicking or going into debt. The more you save, the more secure you'll feel. And once your emergency fund is fully built, you'll have one less thing to worry about in your financial life.

Key Takeaways and Next Steps

- **Start Small, Think Big**: Saving doesn't need to start with large amounts. Even setting aside just $25 a month is a great start. Small, consistent contributions add up over time and lead to bigger savings goals.
- **Build an Emergency Fund**: Aim to save at least three to six months' worth of living expenses. Start small, but make it a priority. Having a safety net helps you avoid going into debt when the unexpected happens.
- **Set Clear, Specific Goals**: Whether it's saving for a vacation, a new car, or your future, specific goals will give you something to work toward and keep you motivated. Break down big goals into smaller, manageable targets to stay on track.
- **Automate Your Savings**: Set up automatic transfers so you're saving without thinking about it. Treat your savings like a bill that gets paid every month.

- **Save for Retirement Early**: The earlier you start saving for retirement, the better. Even small contributions to a retirement account like a 401(k) or IRA can grow over time with compound interest.

Next Steps to Take Today:

1. **Use the Savings Goal Worksheet** to set a specific, realistic savings target. Break it down into monthly goals that feel manageable.

2. **Start an Emergency Fund**: Aim to save $500 in the next 3 months for unexpected expenses. Once you hit that target, aim for 3-6 months of living expenses.

3. **Automate Your Savings**: Set up an automatic transfer to a high-yield savings account. Even $10-$20 a week can add up.

4. **Track Your Progress**: Review your budget and savings regularly. Celebrate milestones along the way, and adjust your savings goals as your income grows.

Saving money is an important first step, but what about managing the money you already have? Credit and debit cards play a crucial role in everyday financial decisions. In the next chapter, we'll explore how to use these cards responsibly, the impact they can have on your financial future, and the importance of managing your credit score.

📍 Savings Tip:

Start by building a small emergency fund—just $500 can cover most unexpected expenses and prevent you from relying on credit cards.

Mastering Digital Payments and Modern Financial Tools

"In the digital age, managing your money is easier than ever—but only if you use the right tools." ~ Anonymous

Gone are the days of carrying cash and writing checks for every expense. Today, managing your money has become faster, easier, and more accessible with digital financial tools. From budgeting apps to payment services and investing platforms, these tools can help you stay on top of your finances, make smarter money moves, and even build wealth over time.

Digital Tools for Budgeting:

- **Mint**: One of the most popular budgeting tools, Mint connects to your bank accounts and credit cards to automatically track and categorize your spending. You can create custom budgets, set savings goals, and get reminders when bills are due.
- **YNAB** (You Need a Budget): YNAB is ideal for people who want to get proactive about their money. It focuses on giving every dollar a job, helping you plan ahead for expenses and track your financial progress.

Digital Payment Tools:

- **Venmo, PayPal, and Cash App**: These payment apps make it easy to send and receive money digitally. Whether you're paying for dinner, splitting rent, or sending a gift, these apps simplify everyday transactions.
- **Apple Pay / Google Pay**: These digital wallets allow you to store credit and debit cards on your phone and pay securely at stores or online without needing your physical card.

Investing Tools:

- **Acorns**: Acorns is a micro-investing app that rounds up your everyday purchases and invests the change into a diversified portfolio. It's a great way to start investing without needing a large lump sum of money.
- **Robinhood**: For those who want more control over their investments, Robinhood offers a user-friendly platform for buying stocks, ETFs, and even cryptocurrencies without commission fees.

Why You Should Use Digital Tools:

- **Convenience**: Digital tools save time and effort. You don't have to manually track every transaction or worry about losing receipts.
- **Transparency**: Apps like Mint give you a clear, real-time overview of your spending, which helps you make informed decisions.
- **Automation**: Tools like Acorns or automatic bill pay help you save without thinking about it and ensure that your payments are made on time.

With the right tools, you can streamline your financial life, save more effectively, and take control of your financial future.

With your budget in place, it's time to focus on two essential areas: saving money and managing debt. A solid budget not only helps you track your spending but also sets the stage for building an emergency fund and setting aside money for your future goals. As we explore the importance of saving, we'll also tackle the subject of debt, showing you how to manage and pay it off efficiently. Together, these strategies will give you more control over your finances and help you build a path to financial freedom.

Chapter 3: Credit and Debit Cards

Understanding Credit and Debit Cards

"Credit is a trust, and trust must be earned." ~ Unknown

Credit and debit cards are a part of almost everyone's daily life, but understanding how they work is crucial for making smart financial decisions. Whether you're swiping your card for a coffee or using it for big-ticket items, knowing how credit and debit cards affect your finances will help you make choices that keep your money—and your credit—healthy.

In this chapter, we'll break down the basics of **credit** and **debit** cards. We'll cover how to use them responsibly, avoid debt, and build good credit for the future. It's all about understanding these tools and making them work for you, rather than the other way around.

Credit Cards vs. Debit Cards: What's the Difference?

It's easy to confuse **credit cards** with **debit cards** because they both allow you to make purchases without cash. But they work very differently.

Debit Cards:

- A **debit card** is linked directly to your checking account, so when you use it, the money is withdrawn from your available balance.
- **Pros**: You can only spend what you have, so there's less risk of going into debt. It's a great tool for managing everyday purchases and staying within your budget.

- **Cons**: Some debit cards don't come with great rewards or perks, and if your account gets compromised, it could take time to resolve, especially if it's a fraudulent transaction.

Credit Cards:
- A **credit card** is essentially a loan from the bank. When you use it, you're borrowing money that you'll need to pay back, usually with interest.
- **Pros**: If used responsibly, credit cards can help you build your **credit score**, which is crucial for securing loans or a mortgage in the future. Plus, many cards offer rewards like cash back or travel points.
- **Cons**: If you carry a balance, the interest can add up quickly, making your purchases much more expensive. If you miss payments, it could also hurt your credit score.

How to Use Credit Cards Responsibly

Credit cards can be a great tool, but they can also lead to financial problems if not used wisely. Here's how to use credit cards responsibly:

Pay Your Balance in Full Every Month

One of the biggest mistakes people make with credit cards is not paying off their balance in full each month. This can lead to accumulating interest, and before you know it, you're paying much more for your purchases than you originally intended.

- **Tip**: If possible, always pay your full credit card balance each month. That way, you avoid paying interest on your purchases.

Know Your Credit Limit

Your **credit limit** is the maximum amount you can spend on your card. It's important to know your credit limit and avoid spending too close to it. Spending too much of your available credit can hurt your credit score and increase your debt.

- **Tip**: Try to keep your credit card balance under 30% of your credit limit. For example, if your limit is $1,000, aim to keep your balance under $300.

Avoid Late Payments

Late payments can lead to hefty fees and damage your credit score, making it harder to borrow money in the future. Set reminders or automate your payments to ensure you never miss a due date.

- **Tip**: Set up automatic payments for at least the minimum payment to avoid late fees.

Understand Your Interest Rates

Credit card companies often charge high-interest rates on any balance that carries over from month to month. The average credit card interest rate is over 20%—which can make debt snowball quickly.

- **Tip**: Pay off your credit card balance as soon as possible to avoid high-interest charges.

Building Your Credit with Credit Cards

A good credit score is essential for many financial milestones, such as getting a car loan or mortgage. Here's how using a credit card wisely can help you build your credit score:

How Credit Scores Work

Your credit score is a number that shows how reliable you are at paying back borrowed money. A higher score means you're less risky to lenders, and they're more likely to approve you for loans with favorable terms.

Credit scores are determined by several factors:

1. **Payment history** (35%): Do you pay your bills on time?
2. **Credit utilization** (30%): How much of your available credit are you using?
3. **Length of credit history** (15%): How long have you had credit accounts?
4. **Types of credit** (10%): Do you have a mix of credit cards, loans, etc.?
5. **New credit inquiries** (10%): Have you recently applied for a lot of credit?

Using Your Credit Card to Build Credit

Using a credit card responsibly can help improve your credit score. Here's how:

- **Pay your bill on time**: This is the most important factor in building good credit.
- **Keep your balance low**: Don't max out your credit card. Keep your balance under 30% of your credit limit.

- **Don't open too many new accounts**: Too many inquiries on your credit report can hurt your score. Stick with the cards you have and use them wisely.

How to Avoid Common Credit Card Mistakes

It's easy to make mistakes with credit cards, especially when you're just starting out. Here are a few common mistakes and how to avoid them:

Only Paying the Minimum Balance

When you only make the minimum payment, you're only paying off the interest and a small part of your balance. This makes it harder to pay off your debt.

- **Tip**: Always pay more than the minimum payment whenever possible. Paying more will help you pay off your balance faster and reduce the interest you pay.

Maxing Out Your Credit Limit

Maxing out your credit card can hurt your credit score and make it harder to pay off your debt.

- **Tip**: Keep your balance low and never exceed your credit limit. If you're approaching your limit, try to pay it down before making more purchases.

Applying for Too Many Cards at Once

Each time you apply for a new credit card, it can cause a hard inquiry on your credit report, which can lower your credit score temporarily.

- **Tip**: Only apply for credit cards when you really need them, and avoid applying for several at once.

Credit Card Rewards: How to Make Them Work for You

Many credit cards offer rewards, such as cash back, points, or miles, for every dollar you spend. These rewards can be great, but you need to use them strategically.

Types of Rewards Cards:

1. **Cash Back**: Earn a percentage of your purchases back in cash. This can be used to pay down your balance or saved for something else.
2. **Travel Rewards**: Earn miles or points that can be redeemed for travel expenses, like flights and hotel stays.
3. **Store-Specific Rewards**: Some credit cards offer discounts or rewards at specific retailers.

How to Make the Most of Your Rewards:

- **Pay your balance in full**: This way, you'll earn rewards without paying interest.
- **Choose a rewards card that fits your lifestyle**: If you travel a lot, a travel rewards card might be best. If you want to earn cash back, go for a card with a strong cash-back program.

Key Takeaways

- **Understand the difference** between credit and debit cards. Debit cards take money directly from your account, while credit cards are loans you pay back later.

- **Use credit cards responsibly**: Pay your balance in full, know your credit limit, and avoid late payments.

- **Build your credit** by using your credit card wisely: Keep your balance low, make timely payments, and avoid opening too many new accounts.

- **Avoid common mistakes** like only paying the minimum balance or maxing out your credit card.

- **Make the most of rewards**: Use rewards cards wisely, pay off your balance, and choose a card that fits your lifestyle.

Next Steps:

1. **Check your current credit situation**: Use a free credit report tool to check your current credit score and understand how credit cards are impacting it.

2. **Choose a credit card**: If you don't already have one, research the best credit cards for your lifestyle and financial goals.

3. **Start using your card responsibly**: Begin using your credit card for small purchases and pay off the balance in full each month to build good credit.

Overall, a bad credit score can limit your financial options, increase your costs, and even affect your quality of life. Improving and maintaining a good credit score can help you save money, access better financial opportunities, and achieve greater financial stability.

Now that you understand how credit cards work and how to use them responsibly, it's time to talk about an equally important aspect of your financial journey: **paying off debt**. Whether it's credit card debt, student loans, or other forms of borrowing, paying off debt is essential for achieving long-term financial freedom.

Using credit responsibly is a great first step, but what happens if you've already accumulated some debt? Don't worry—you're not alone, and the good news is that it's possible to get back on track. In this next section, we'll dive into strategies for tackling debt effectively. We'll cover practical tips, like the **Debt Snowball** and **Debt Avalanche** methods, that can help you pay off debt faster while avoiding common pitfalls.

Paying Off Debt: A Game Plan

Debt can feel overwhelming, especially when you're just starting to build your financial future. Credit card debt can be a huge issue for young adults. Understanding the financial landscape for individuals aged 18 to 25 is crucial, as this group often faces unique debt challenges.

Here are some key statistics:
- **Average Debt**: As of 2024, the average non-mortgage debt for individuals aged 18 to 29 is approximately $12,871. Debt.org
- **Credit Card Debt**: Members of Generation Z (ages 18–26) carry an average credit card debt of $3,148, which is notably lower than that of older generations. Synchrony
- **Student Loan Debt**: In 2021, approximately 7.8 million Americans aged 18 to 25 held student loan debt, with an average balance nearing $15,000. Wikipedia

- **Debt-to-Income Ratio**: The debt-to-income ratio for individuals aged 18 to 29 is about 22%, indicating that young adults allocate a significant portion of their income to debt repayment.

But don't worry! With the right strategies and mindset, you can take control of your debt and set yourself up for financial freedom. Let's break down how to pay off debt efficiently and responsibly.

Step 1: Know What You Owe
Before you can make a plan to pay off your debt, you need to know exactly how much you owe. This includes all debts, from student loans to credit card balances, car loans, and even any unpaid bills.

Actionable Tip:
- **List all your debts**: Write down the balance, interest rate, and minimum monthly payment for each debt.
- **Prioritize high-interest debt**: Credit cards usually have higher interest rates than student loans, so it's important to pay these off faster.

Step 2: Create a Debt Payoff Strategy
Once you know what you owe, it's time to choose a debt repayment method. The two most popular methods are the **Debt Snowball** and **Debt Avalanche** strategies.

- **Debt Snowball Method**: Pay off your smallest debt first. Once it's gone, move on to the next smallest debt, and so on. This method is great for motivation because you see progress quickly. **Example**: If you owe $500 on a credit card and $5,000 on a student loan, focus on paying off the $500 credit card first. Once that's gone, you can put all that money toward the next smallest debt.

- **Debt Avalanche Method**: Focus on paying off the debt with the highest interest rate first. This method saves you money in the long run, but it may take longer to see progress. **Example**: If you have credit card debt with a 20% interest rate and a student loan with a 4% interest rate, you would pay off the credit card debt first, because it's costing you more in interest.

Actionable Tip:

- **Choose the method that works best for you**: If you're motivated by quick wins, try the Debt Snowball. If you're focused on saving money, go with the Debt Avalanche.

Step 3: Create a Budget that Supports Debt Payoff

To pay off debt, you need to make room in your budget. This might mean cutting back on discretionary spending (like eating out or buying the latest tech) and putting more money toward paying off your debt.

Actionable Tip:

- **Cut back on non-essential spending**: Track your expenses for a month and find areas to cut back. Even small sacrifices can add up to big savings over time.
- **Automate your payments**: Set up automatic transfers to ensure you're consistently putting money toward your debt.

Step 4: Look for Extra Income

If you're not able to pay off your debt quickly with your current income, consider finding ways to make extra money. This could be through a side hustle, selling unused items, or even picking up additional shifts at your current job.

Actionable Tip:

- **Explore side gigs**: Many 20-year-olds earn extra cash by tutoring, delivering food, freelancing, or using their talents for things like graphic design or writing.
- **Start small**: Even adding $50 or $100 a month to your debt payments can make a big difference over time.

Step 5: Stay Consistent and Track Your Progress

Consistency is key when it comes to paying off debt. Celebrate small milestones along the way to keep your motivation high. Whether it's paying off a credit card or reaching a debt-free month, every step forward is a win!

Actionable Tip:

- **Use a debt tracker**: Visual tools, like a debt tracker or app, can help you see how much progress you've made. Apps like Mint or YNAB allow you to track debt and visualize your goals.

Step 6: Avoid Taking on New Debt

While paying off your current debt, it's important to avoid accumulating more debt. Stay disciplined with your spending and build a buffer in your budget for unexpected expenses.

Actionable Tip:

- **Use credit cards responsibly**: If you must use credit cards, always pay off the balance in full each month to avoid paying interest. If that's too hard, consider using a debit card or prepaying for things with cash.

Step 7: Celebrate Your Success!

Once you've paid off your debt, take a moment to celebrate your achievement. This is a huge milestone in your financial journey and shows that you can take control of your financial future.

Actionable Tip:

- **Reinvest in yourself**: Use the money you were spending on debt payments to build an emergency fund, invest for the future, or save for your next big goal.

Real-Life Example:

Meet *Jordan*, a 21-year-old recent college grad. Jordan has $2,000 in credit card debt at 18% interest and $8,000 in student loans at 4%. Jordan decides to use the **Debt Avalanche Method**, putting all extra funds toward the credit card debt while paying the minimum on the student loans.

By cutting back on dining out and picking up a weekend side gig, Jordan is able to put an extra $300 toward the credit card each month. In just seven months, Jordan pays off the credit card debt. The $300 previously going to credit card payments is now used to accelerate the student loan payments, allowing Jordan to pay off the loan faster and save money on interest in the long run.

Remember - debt doesn't have to control your life. With discipline, a clear strategy, and a little patience, you can pay off your debt and move toward financial freedom. Start now, and you'll thank yourself later.

📍 Debt Repayment Tip:

The Debt Avalanche Method saves you more money over time, as it focuses on paying off high-interest debts first. But the Debt Snowball Method works for people who need small wins to stay motivated.

Adjust Your Plan When Life Changes

Your financial situation is likely to change as you move through different stages of life. Whether it's a new job, a pay raise, unexpected expenses, or even a change in your financial goals, learning how to adapt your debt repayment plan is crucial for staying on track. Here's how to make adjustments to your plan when life throws you a curveball:

Adjusting Your Plan After a Pay Raise or Job Change

When you get a raise, promotion, or even a new job that pays more, it's tempting to increase your lifestyle spending—dining out more often, buying new clothes, or splurging on gadgets. But if you're serious about paying off debt, the best thing you can do is redirect some (or all) of that extra income toward your debt repayment plan.

Actionable Tip:

- **Increase your debt payments**: Aim to put at least 50% of your raise or new income toward paying off your debts. This will help you make more significant progress, especially if you've been working on a method like the Debt Avalanche, which focuses on paying off high-interest debt first.
- **Avoid lifestyle inflation**: Try to maintain the same lifestyle you had before the raise. Instead of spending more on discretionary items, channel that extra cash toward accelerating your debt payoff.

Dealing with Unexpected Expenses

Life happens, and sometimes expenses come out of nowhere—whether it's a medical emergency, a car repair, or an unplanned trip. If you find yourself in a situation where you can't make your regular debt payments, don't panic. Here's how to handle the situation:

Actionable Tip:

- **Review your budget**: Take a look at your current expenses and see where you can cut back. Even small sacrifices, like skipping dining out for a few weeks or reducing your entertainment budget, can free up money to put toward your debt.

- **Prioritize your debt payments**: If you're facing a temporary cash flow issue, try to make the minimum payments on all your debts to avoid penalties. If you can, prioritize the debts with the highest interest rates to minimize the amount of interest you'll accrue.

- **Consider temporary forbearance**: If you're unable to make the minimum payments, reach out to your creditors. Many lenders offer forbearance or deferment options, allowing you to temporarily pause or reduce payments without facing penalties.

Adjusting Your Plan After Major Life Events

Life events like moving to a new city, graduating from college, or even getting married can have a significant impact on your finances. These events may lead to a shift in your income or expenses, so it's important to reassess your debt repayment plan.

Actionable Tip:

- **Reevaluate your priorities**: For example, if you're moving to a new city and your living expenses will increase, consider adjusting your debt payments temporarily to accommodate your new cost of living.

- **Track your spending closely**: During life transitions, it's easy to let spending get out of hand. Use budgeting apps or spreadsheets to track every expense so that you can make informed decisions about where to cut back if needed.

What to Do If You're Struggling to Stay on Track

If you find that your debt payoff plan isn't working as expected—whether it's because you're falling behind, have missed a few payments, or aren't seeing the progress you'd like—it's time to take a step back and reassess.

Actionable Tip:

- **Simplify your plan**: If the plan feels overwhelming, consider simplifying your approach. Focus on paying off one debt at a time (using the Debt Snowball method) or revisit your budget to make sure you're allocating enough money to your debt each month.
- **Look for other sources of income**: If your current job isn't providing enough flexibility to make larger payments, consider looking for side gigs or freelance work. Every little bit helps when it comes to paying down debt faster.
- **Seek professional help**: If your debt feels unmanageable, consider reaching out to a financial counselor or debt management professional. They can help you come up with a revised plan and even negotiate with creditors on your behalf.

Make Adjustments to Your Goals Over Time

As your financial situation improves, you might find that you can pay off debt faster than expected, or you might want to shift focus to other financial goals, such as saving for a big purchase, starting an investment plan, or building an emergency fund.

Actionable Tip:

- **Set new goals**: Once you've paid off your high-interest debt, set new goals for savings and investing. The more you adjust your plan and remain flexible, the more successful you'll be in the long run.

- **Track progress regularly**: Set a monthly or quarterly check-in to track your debt repayment progress and reassess your budget, income, and goals. Regularly reviewing your plan can keep you motivated and focused on your objectives.

By learning how to adjust your debt repayment plan, you'll be better prepared to handle changes in your financial situation and keep moving toward a debt-free future. Remember, flexibility is key, and it's better to adapt your plan than to get discouraged by unexpected changes.

Key Takeaways:

- **Know the difference** between credit cards (borrowed money with interest) and debit cards (money you already have).

- **Credit cards can build credit**, but if not managed responsibly, they can lead to high-interest debt. Always aim to pay off your balance in full each month.

- **Understanding your credit score** is crucial—it affects your ability to borrow money and the interest rates you'll pay.

- **Debt Repayment Methods**: The Debt Snowball (smallest debt first) and Debt Avalanche (highest interest debt first) methods help you stay focused and motivated to pay off debt.

- **Avoid lifestyle inflation**: As your income increases, resist the urge to upgrade your lifestyle. Instead, focus on paying down debt and saving for your future.

Now that you have a solid understanding of credit and debit cards, it's time to look at how taxes fit into the bigger picture of your finances. From your paycheck to your annual tax filings, taxes can affect everything from your savings to your spending. In the next chapter, we'll break down the basics of taxes and what you need to know to keep more of your hard-earned money.

Fixing Your Credit Score and Breaking Free from Credit Card Dependency

Having a poor credit score can significantly impact your financial life, making it challenging to secure loans, rent an apartment, or even get a job. If you're looking to fix your credit score and move away from relying on credit cards, here's a comprehensive guide to help you achieve both goals.

Step 1: Obtain Your Credit Report

The first step in fixing your credit score is to obtain your credit report from all three major credit bureaus: Experian, TransUnion, and Equifax. You're entitled to one free report from each bureau annually through AnnualCreditReport.com. Review these reports for errors, late payments, or accounts you don't recognize. Dispute any inaccuracies you find, as they can drag down your score.

Step 2: Understand Your Credit Score Factors

Your credit score is calculated based on several factors, including payment history, credit utilization, length of credit history, new credit inquiries, and types of credit accounts. Understanding these factors can help you focus on what to improve. For example, late payments can hurt your score, so prioritize paying your bills on time moving forward.

Step 3: Pay Down Existing Debt

If you have outstanding credit card debt, work on paying it down aggressively. Start with high-interest cards first, as they cost you more in the long run. Consider using the debt snowball method, where you pay off the smallest debts first for psychological wins, or the avalanche method, which focuses on the highest interest rates. Aim to reduce your credit utilization ratio (the amount of credit you're using compared to your total credit limit) to below 30% for a positive impact on your score.

Step 4: Set Up Payment Reminders

To avoid late payments, set up automatic payments for bills and credit card minimums. You can also use calendar reminders to keep track of due dates. Consistent, on-time payments can significantly improve your credit score over time.

Step 5: Limit New Credit Applications

Each time you apply for new credit, a hard inquiry is made on your report, which can temporarily lower your score. Avoid applying for new credit cards while you're in the process of fixing your credit.

Step 6: Consider Alternatives to Credit Cards

To stop relying on credit cards, consider using a debit card or cash for everyday purchases. This approach encourages you to stick to your budget, as you can only spend what you have. If you want to build credit without credit cards, consider a secured credit card or a credit-builder loan, which allows you to establish a positive credit history while minimizing the risk of overspending.

Step 7: Monitor Your Progress

Regularly check your credit score to monitor your progress. Many banks and financial institutions offer free credit score tracking. Celebrate small victories along the way, and stay committed to your goal of financial stability.

By following these steps, you can fix your credit score while breaking free from the cycle of credit card dependency. A healthier credit profile will open doors to better financial opportunities and a more secure future.

Understanding Banking and Interest

Banking is a fundamental aspect of our financial lives, providing a safe place to store money, access credit, and manage transactions. Whether you're opening a checking account to manage daily expenses, a savings account to build an emergency fund, or taking out a loan to buy a house, understanding how banking works and the role of interest is essential for making informed financial decisions.

The Basics of Banking

At its core, banking is the business of accepting deposits and making loans. Banks offer various types of accounts, including:

Checking Accounts: These accounts are designed for everyday transactions. They allow you to deposit money, withdraw cash, and make payments via checks or debit cards. Checking accounts often come with minimal interest rates, as their primary purpose is to facilitate transactions.

Savings Accounts: Unlike checking accounts, savings accounts are designed to help you save money over time. They typically offer higher interest rates, encouraging you to set aside funds for future expenses or emergencies. The interest earned on a savings account can contribute to your savings growth, albeit at a relatively modest rate.

Certificates of Deposit (CDs): CDs are time deposits that offer higher interest rates than regular savings accounts in exchange for locking in your money for a specified term, usually ranging from a few months to several years. Withdrawing money before the term ends may result in penalties, but the trade-off is a guaranteed return on your investment.

Loans and Credit: Banks also provide various loan products, including personal loans, auto loans, and mortgages. When you borrow money, you agree to repay it with interest over a specified period. Understanding the terms of these loans, including interest rates and repayment schedules, is crucial for managing debt responsibly.

The Role of Interest in Banking

"Interest is the rent you pay for the use of someone else's money." ~ Unknown

Interest is a key concept in personal finance that can impact both your savings and your debt. It's essentially the cost of borrowing money (in the case of loans) or the reward you earn for saving money (in the case of savings accounts). Understanding how interest works is critical because it can make or break your financial goals. Let's break it down!

How Interest Works on Debt

When you borrow money—whether it's through a credit card, student loan, car loan, or mortgage—you're charged interest. This is how banks make money by lending you cash. The more you borrow and the longer it takes you to repay the loan, the more interest you'll pay.

How is Interest Calculated?

Interest can be calculated in two main ways: **simple interest** and **compound interest**.

- **Simple Interest**: You're charged interest on the amount you borrowed (the principal). The formula looks like this:

  Interest = Principal × Interest Rate × Time

- **Compound Interest**: This is when interest is charged on both the principal **and** any interest that has already been added. Compound interest is how banks and credit card companies make money more quickly because you're charged interest on your previous interest.

Example of Interest on Debt (Credit Cards)

Let's say you have a **credit card balance** of $1,000 with an interest rate of 18% per year. If you don't pay it off for a full year, here's how the interest works out:

- **Simple Interest Example**:
  - Interest = $1,000 × 18% × 1 year = $180.
  - So, after one year, you would owe $1,180 if you didn't pay anything off.
- **Compound Interest Example** (assuming interest compounds monthly):
  - Interest is calculated not just on the initial $1,000 but on any interest that accrues over the months.
  - At the end of one year, the total amount you owe would be **higher than $1,180** because of the compounding effect.

Tip: Credit cards often compound interest daily or monthly, so the longer you carry a balance, the more you'll owe in interest. This can make a small debt grow quickly if you're not careful.

How Interest Works on Savings

Just like how interest works in your favor when you have debt, it also works in your favor when you save money. Banks pay you interest for keeping your money with them in a savings account. This is their way of thanking you for letting them use your money to lend out to others.

How is Interest Calculated on Savings?

Just like with debt, interest on savings can be calculated with either simple or compound interest. Most banks use **compound interest** for savings accounts, which means the interest you earn gets added to your balance, and you earn interest on that interest.

Example of Interest on Savings (High-Yield Savings Account)

Let's say you open a **high-yield savings account** with a balance of $1,000 and an interest rate of 2% per year. If the interest compounds monthly, here's how your balance would grow:

- **First Month**: Interest = $1,000 × 2% ÷ 12 = $1.67.
  Now, your new balance is $1,001.67.
- **After One Year** (with compounding):
  The total interest earned over 12 months would be **around $20.20**, making your balance $1,020.20.

The more money you have in your savings account and the longer you keep it there, the more interest you'll earn.

The Importance of Interest Rates

The interest rate—whether on a loan or a savings account—can make a huge difference in your financial health. Here's why:

- **High-interest rates on debt** mean you'll pay more over time. This is especially important to consider with credit cards, payday loans, or other high-interest loans.
- **Low-interest rates on savings** mean your money grows more slowly. However, with **high-yield savings accounts** or **certificates of deposit (CDs)**, you can earn a better return on your savings.

Example: Saving vs. Borrowing

- **Saving**: If you deposit $1,000 in a savings account with an interest rate of 2%, after one year, you'd earn $20 in interest.
- **Borrowing**: If you borrow $1,000 at an interest rate of 18% on a credit card, after one year, you could owe $180 in interest—assuming you don't pay off the balance.

The key takeaway? **The higher the interest rate on debt, the more expensive it becomes**. On the flip side, **the higher the interest rate on savings, the more your money grows**.

How to Manage Interest Effectively

1. **Pay off high-interest debt quickly**: If you have debt with a high interest rate, especially credit cards, it's essential to pay it off as soon as possible. The longer you carry the balance, the more you'll end up paying in interest.

2. **Shop for the best savings rates**: Look for high-yield savings accounts or investment options that offer better interest rates to make your money grow faster.

3. **Understand your rates**: Whether it's a loan or a savings account, always know the interest rate you're dealing with. For loans, look for the **APR** (annual percentage rate) to understand the true cost of borrowing.

4. **Consider debt consolidation**: If you have multiple high-interest debts, consolidating them into one loan with a lower interest rate can help reduce the overall interest you pay.

Key Takeaways

- **Interest on debt** can make borrowed money more expensive, especially if it compounds over time.
- **Compound interest on savings** helps your money grow, but it's important to shop for accounts with high interest rates to maximize your return.
- **Pay off high-interest debt** as quickly as possible to avoid paying excessive interest.
- **Look for ways to earn more interest on your savings**, such as using high-yield savings accounts.

By understanding common banking fees and implementing strategies to manage them, you can avoid unnecessary costs and maximize your savings. Being proactive about your banking practices not only saves you money but also enhances your overall financial literacy. As you navigate the world of banking, staying informed and making smart choices can significantly impact your financial health and help you achieve your financial goals.

Once you've got a grip on saving and managing debt, it's important to understand how **taxes** affect your income and expenses. While taxes may seem complicated, having a basic understanding of them can save you money and prevent unexpected surprises.

In this chapter, we'll break down the fundamentals of taxes, explain key terms, and offer tips on how to make taxes work in your favor. By understanding your tax responsibilities, you'll feel more confident in managing your finances.

Chapter 4: Introduction to Taxes

Taxes Made Simple: What They Are and How They Affect You

"In this world, nothing is certain except death and taxes." ~ Benjamin Franklin

Taxes. The word alone can make anyone cringe, but understanding them is essential to managing your finances. Whether it's a portion of your paycheck being deducted or filing your annual return, taxes are part of life. But don't worry—by the end of this chapter, you'll have a clearer understanding of how taxes work, why they matter, and how to make them work for you (or at least not against you!).

In this chapter, we'll cover the basics of income taxes, explain how your paycheck is affected by taxes, and give you some tips on how to minimize what you owe and maximize your refunds. Taxes may seem complicated, but once you break them down into manageable chunks, they're a lot easier to handle.

What Are Taxes and Why Do We Pay Them?

Simply put, **taxes** are money that governments take from individuals and businesses to fund public services. This could include anything from paying for roads and schools to funding national defense or social security programs. The government uses taxes to run and maintain the services that keep society functioning.

Types of Taxes:

There are a few different types of taxes that you might encounter:

1. **Income Tax**: This is the most common tax, and it's taken from your paycheck. It's based on how much money you make. The more you earn, the more income tax you pay.
2. **Sales Tax**: This is a percentage added to the price of goods and services when you make a purchase. It varies by state and city.
3. **Property Tax**: If you own property (like a house or land), you'll pay property taxes. These taxes are typically assessed by local governments and go toward funding public services in your area.
4. **Social Security and Medicare Taxes**: These taxes are taken out of your paycheck to fund Social Security (for retirement benefits) and Medicare (for healthcare for seniors).

How Income Tax Works

Most of us are familiar with **income tax**, but it's still one of the most confusing parts of the tax system. Here's the deal:

What is Taxable Income?

Your **taxable income** is the amount of money you earn that is subject to taxation. This includes things like your salary, wages, tips, and any other income you earn. However, there are things that can reduce your taxable income, like:

- **Deductions** (for things like student loan interest, mortgage interest, and medical expenses)
- **Credits** (for things like education expenses or child care)

How is Income Tax Calculated?

Income tax is usually **progressive**, meaning that the more you earn, the higher the percentage of taxes you pay. In the U.S., income tax is divided into **brackets**, with each bracket representing a different tax rate. The higher your income, the more you pay in taxes.

For example, in the U.S., the tax brackets in 2024 (for a single filer) look something like this:

- **10%** on income up to $11,000
- **12%** on income from $11,001 to $44,725
- **22%** on income from $44,726 to $95,375
- **24%** on income from $95,376 to $182,100
- **32%** on income from $182,101 to $231,250
- **35%** on income from $231,251 to $578,100
- **37%** on income over $578,101

The key thing to understand is that you **don't pay the same tax rate on all your income**. Instead, you pay the lowest rate on your first dollar of income and the higher rates on your income above certain thresholds.

Example:

Let's say you're a single filer and earn $50,000 a year. Here's how your taxes might break down:

- The first $11,000 is taxed at 10%.
- The next $33,725 (from $11,001 to $44,725) is taxed at 12%.
- The remaining $5,275 (from $44,726 to $50,000) is taxed at 22%.

You wouldn't pay 22% on your entire $50,000 income. Instead, you'd pay 10%, 12%, and 22% on different portions of your income.

How Your Paycheck Is Affected by Taxes

When you start a job, your employer will withhold a portion of your paycheck for federal income taxes. This is how it works:

- **W-4 Form**: When you start a job, you'll fill out a **W-4 form**. This form tells your employer how much tax to withhold based on your filing status (single, married, etc.) and how many allowances you claim. Click here to see what the form looks like.
- **Withholding**: Your employer uses the W-4 to withhold federal income tax, Social Security, and Medicare taxes from your paycheck.
- **State and Local Taxes**: Depending on where you live, state and local taxes might also be withheld from your paycheck.

Here's a quick breakdown of what you'll see on your pay stub:
- **Gross income**: Your total earnings before taxes.
- **Deductions**: The portion of your income that's taken out for federal, state, and local taxes, Social Security, and Medicare.
- **Net income**: What's left after all the deductions. This is what gets deposited into your account.

Example:

Let's say you earn $3,000 a month and are single. Based on your W-4, here's an example of how your paycheck might look after taxes:
- **Gross income**: $3,000
- **Federal tax withholding**: $250
- **State tax withholding**: $100
- **Social Security**: $186
- **Medicare**: $43.50
- **Net income**: $2,420.50

So, even though your gross income is $3,000, you'll receive $2,420.50 after taxes and deductions.

Tax Deductions and Credits

When it comes to taxes, understanding **deductions** and **credits** can help you keep more of your money. Both can lower your tax bill, but they work in different ways.

Tax Deductions

A **deduction** reduces your **taxable income**, meaning you pay taxes on a lower amount. Common deductions include:

- **Student loan interest**: If you're paying off student loans, you can deduct up to $2,500 of interest you've paid.
- **Mortgage interest**: Homeowners can deduct interest paid on their mortgage, potentially lowering their taxable income.
- **Charitable donations**: Donations to qualified charities can also reduce your taxable income.

Tax Credits

A **credit** directly reduces the **amount of tax you owe**. Unlike deductions, credits reduce your tax bill dollar-for-dollar. Some common credits include:

- **Earned Income Tax Credit (EITC)**: For low to moderate-income workers, this credit can provide a substantial refund.
- **Child Tax Credit**: If you have children under 17, you can claim up to $2,000 per child to reduce your taxes.
- **American Opportunity Credit**: This credit helps offset costs for the first four years of post-secondary education, up to $2,500.

Quick Tip:

To maximize your deductions and credits, keep track of receipts, charitable donations, and tuition payments throughout the year. The more you track, the easier it will be to claim the deductions and credits that apply to you when tax season rolls around.

Filing Your Taxes

At the end of the year, you'll file your tax return to report your income, deductions, and credits. If too much was withheld from your paycheck, you might get a refund. If too little was withheld, you'll owe additional taxes.

- **Forms**: The main form for filing your taxes is the **1040**. If you have simpler tax situations, you might be able to file with a free online tool or software like TurboTax or Credit Karma. Click here to see what the Form 1040 looks like.
- **When to File**: The deadline for filing your taxes is typically **April 15th** each year. If you miss the deadline, you may face penalties and interest on any unpaid taxes.

Key Takeaways

- **Taxes are essential** for funding public services, and you'll pay them on your income, purchases, and property.
- **Income tax** is the most common type, and it's based on how much you earn.
- **Taxable income** is the amount of money you earn that is subject to tax, and it can be reduced by deductions and credits.
- **Deductions** lower your taxable income, while **credits** directly reduce the taxes you owe.
- **Your paycheck is taxed** based on the information you provide on your W-4, and the taxes are automatically withheld.

Next Steps

1. **Review your W-4 form**: Make sure it's up to date and accurately reflects your tax situation.

2. **Track your deductions**: Keep records of potential deductions, like student loan interest, mortgage payments, or medical expenses, to reduce your taxable income.

3. **Prepare for tax season**: Use a tax preparation tool or meet with a tax professional to file your taxes accurately and maximize your refund.

As you continue to solidify your financial foundation, it's essential to consider how **insurance** fits into your overall financial plan. Insurance can provide a safety net in case of unexpected events, helping you avoid financial setbacks that could derail your progress. In this chapter, we'll explore the different types of insurance you need—whether it's for health, car, renters, or life—and help you understand how to choose the right coverage to protect yourself and your loved ones.

 Tax Time Reminder:

Set aside some time to gather your documents early in the year (W-2s, receipts, etc.). Waiting until the last minute can lead to stress or missed deductions.

Chapter 5: Insurance

Insurance 101: Protecting Your Future

"An ounce of prevention is worth a pound of cure." ~ Benjamin Franklin

Insurance isn't the most exciting topic, but it's an important part of managing your finances and protecting yourself from life's unexpected events. Whether it's health issues, car accidents, or damage to your home, having the right insurance can keep you from being financially overwhelmed when something goes wrong.

In this chapter, we'll break down the basics of insurance—what it is, why you need it, and how to choose the right policies for your situation. You'll learn about different types of insurance (like health, auto, renters, and life) and how they help provide a safety net for you and your loved ones.

What is Insurance and Why Do You Need It?

In simple terms, **insurance** is a way to protect yourself financially against unexpected events. You pay a regular amount (called a **premium**) to an insurance company, and in return, they cover certain costs if something bad happens—like getting into an accident, needing medical care, or losing your belongings in a fire.

Without insurance, you'd have to pay for these costs out of pocket, which could quickly become unaffordable. Insurance helps share that risk, so you're not left facing massive bills on your own.

How Insurance Works

Let's say you have a car accident. The cost to repair your car could be thousands of dollars. Without insurance, you'd have to pay for it all yourself. But if you have auto insurance, you'll only have to pay a small amount (your deductible), and the insurance company will cover the rest.

- **Premium**: The amount you pay regularly (usually monthly) to keep your insurance coverage active.
- **Deductible**: The amount you pay out of pocket before the insurance company starts covering the costs.
- **Coverage**: What's actually covered by the insurance policy (e.g., car repairs, medical bills, home damage).

Types of Insurance You Need

There are several types of insurance you should consider as you start your adult life. While some may be required by law, others are essential for protecting your financial well-being.

Health Insurance

Health insurance is one of the most important types of insurance you can have. It helps cover medical expenses, from doctor visits and prescription drugs to surgery and emergency care. Without health insurance, medical bills can quickly spiral out of control.

- **Why It's Important**: Healthcare can be very expensive, especially in emergencies. Health insurance helps you avoid the financial strain that comes with unexpected medical costs.
- **What's Covered**: Doctor's visits, hospital stays, prescription drugs, mental health care, and sometimes dental and vision care.

- **How to Choose**: If you're under 26, you can stay on your parents' health insurance plan. If you're on your own, you'll need to either get insurance through your employer or purchase it through the **Health Insurance Marketplace**.

Auto Insurance

If you own a car, auto insurance is required by law in most states. It covers the costs of damage to your vehicle and others in the event of an accident, as well as other situations like theft or natural disasters.

- **Why It's Important**: Car accidents are common, and they can be expensive. Auto insurance protects you from having to pay for repairs, medical bills, or legal fees on your own.
- **What's Covered**: Damage to your car, liability for damage or injury to others, medical expenses, and sometimes even rental car coverage while your car is being repaired.
- **How to Choose**: Depending on your state, you'll need different levels of coverage. Generally, you'll need **liability coverage**, and you may want **collision** or **comprehensive coverage** for extra protection.

Renters Insurance

Even if you don't own your home, **renters insurance** is an essential type of coverage. It protects your belongings in case of damage or theft, and it also provides liability coverage if someone is injured on your property.

- **Why It's Important**: Renters insurance is inexpensive, but it protects you from significant losses. Without it, you'd have to replace stolen or damaged items (like a laptop, phone, or clothes) out of pocket.
- **What's Covered**: Personal property (clothes, electronics, furniture), liability coverage (if someone gets hurt in your

apartment), and additional living expenses if you need to stay somewhere else after an incident like a fire.

- **How to Choose**: Renters insurance is usually cheap—typically between $10-$30 per month. Shop around and compare coverage to find a plan that fits your needs.

Life Insurance

Life insurance helps provide for your loved ones in the event of your death. It can cover funeral costs, pay off debts, or provide income for your family. While life insurance isn't something you may need right away, it becomes more important as you get older, especially if you have dependents or significant debt. You can check this link for the 7 best life insurance companies according to NerdWallet.

- **Why It's Important**: If you have people relying on your income (spouse, kids, etc.), life insurance ensures they're financially supported if something happens to you.
- **What's Covered**: A payout to your beneficiaries upon your death. It can help cover funeral costs, debts, and living expenses for your family.
- **How to Choose**: Consider a **term life insurance policy**, which covers you for a specific number of years (e.g., 10, 20, or 30 years). It's usually more affordable than **whole life insurance**, which provides lifetime coverage and also has an investment component.

How to Choose the Right Insurance

Choosing the right insurance depends on your needs, lifestyle, and budget. Here's how to approach it:

1. **Assess Your Risks**: Think about what could go wrong. Do you drive a lot? Are you in good health? Do you have dependents or a lot of debt? These factors will help you decide what types of insurance you need.

2. **Compare Policies**: Insurance providers often offer different levels of coverage at various price points. Make sure to compare multiple options to find one that fits your budget and needs.

3. **Don't Over-Insure**: While it's important to be covered, you don't need to buy every type of insurance. Focus on the essentials—like health, auto, renters, and possibly life insurance depending on your situation.

4. **Shop for Discounts**: Some providers offer discounts if you bundle your policies (e.g., car and renters insurance with the same company). Look for ways to save without sacrificing coverage.

Key Takeaways

- **Insurance is a safety net** that protects you from financial loss due to unexpected events.

- **Health insurance**, **auto insurance**, **renters insurance**, and **life insurance** are essential types of coverage to consider.

- **Premiums** are the regular payments you make for insurance coverage, and they vary based on your needs and the level of coverage.

- **Deductibles** are the amount you pay out of pocket before your insurance kicks in.

- **Shop around** for the best policies and look for discounts to save money on coverage.

Next Steps

1. **Evaluate your insurance needs**: Make a list of what types of insurance you need based on your lifestyle and financial situation.

2. **Get quotes**: Contact multiple insurance providers to compare premiums, coverage, and benefits.

3. **Review your coverage regularly**: As your life changes (new job, new car, marriage, etc.), revisit your insurance needs to ensure you're still adequately covered.

Insurance Tip:
You may not need every type of insurance, but health, auto, and renters insurance are usually must-haves for financial security.

Quick Fact:
Having good health insurance doesn't just protect you from big medical bills—it can also save you money in the long run by preventing financial strain from even small health issues.

INSURANCE CHECKLIST

Here's a comprehensive checklist for insurance that can help you assess your needs to ensure you have the necessary coverage:

Car Insurance

- ☐ **Assess Your Coverage Needs:** Determine whether you need liability, collision, and comprehensive coverage.

- ☐ **Understand State Requirements:** Research your state's minimum insurance requirements.

- ☐ **Compare Quotes:** Get quotes from multiple insurance providers to find the best rate.

- ☐ **Review Discounts:** Inquire about discounts for safe driving, multiple policies, or vehicle safety features.

- ☐ **Check Your Deductible:** Decide on a deductible amount that fits your budget for out of pocket expenses.

- ☐ **Read the Policy:** Ensure you understand the terms, conditions, and exclusions in your policy.

Health Insurance

- ☐ **Evaluate Your Health Needs:** Consider your current health, frequency of doctor visits, and any ongoing treatments.

- ☐ **Research Available Plans:** Look into employer sponsored plans, government programs, or individual plans.

- ☐ **Check Coverage Options:** Make sure the plan covers essential services like preventive
  care, prescriptions, and specialist visits.
- ☐ **Understand Costs:** Review premiums, deductibles, copays, and out of pocket maximums.
- ☐ **Check Network Providers:** Ensure your preferred doctors and hospitals are in network to avoid extra costs.
- ☐ **Consider Supplemental Insurance:** Look into options like dental, vision, or long term
  care insurance if needed.

Renters Insurance

- ☐ **Inventory Your Belongings:** List valuable items to determine how much coverage you
  need.
- ☐ **Assess Liability Needs:** Decide on the level of liability coverage that would protect you
  against potential lawsuits.
- ☐ **Compare Policies:** Get quotes from various providers to find the best coverage and rates.
- ☐ **Understand Coverage Limits:** Check for limits on specific items, such as electronics or
  jewelry.
- ☐ **Review Policy Exclusions:** Be aware of what is not covered, such as certain natural
  disasters or specific personal items.
- ☐ **Consider Additional Coverage:** Explore options for valuable items or special collections that may require extra coverage.

Pet Insurance

- ☐ **Evaluate Your Pet's Health:** Consider age, breed, and any preexisting conditions when choosing a policy.

- ☐ **Research Insurance Providers:** Look for reputable companies with good customer reviews and claim processes.

- ☐ **Understand Coverage Options:** Review what is covered (e.g., accidents, illnesses, routine care) and what is excluded.

- ☐ **Compare Plans:** Get quotes from multiple insurers to find the best fit for your budget and coverage needs.

- ☐ **Check for Waiting Periods:** Be aware of any waiting periods before coverage begins for specific conditions.

- ☐ **Review the Claims Process:** Understand how to file a claim and the reimbursement process.

Life Insurance

- ☐ **Determine Coverage Amount:** Calculate how much coverage you need based on debts, living expenses, and future goals.

- ☐ **Choose Between Term and Whole Life:** Decide which type of policy aligns with your financial objectives and needs.

- ☐ **Research Providers:** Compare rates and financial strength of different insurance companies.

- ☐ **Understand Policy Terms:** Read the policy details carefully, including exclusions and limitations.

☐ **Consider Riders:** Look into additional options, such as accidental death or critical illness riders, to enhance your policy.

☐ **Review Beneficiary Designations:** Ensure your beneficiaries are correctly designated and kept up to date.

By following this checklist, you can ensure you have the appropriate insurance coverage to protect yourself, your belongings, and your loved ones. Regularly reviewing your insurance policies and making necessary adjustments will help you stay prepared for life's uncertainties.

For many young adults, paying for **college** is one of the biggest financial challenges. Whether you're about to start your college journey or you're figuring out how to pay off student loans, understanding how to finance your education is key.

In the next chapter, we'll explore various options for paying for college, from scholarships and grants to student loans and budgeting tips. With the right strategies in place, you can make the cost of college more manageable and set yourself up for success.

Chapter 6: Paying For College

Understanding Costs And Funding Options

"The investment in knowledge pays the best interest." ~ Benjamin Franklin

Going to college is a big step—and often, a big financial commitment. Whether you're just starting to explore your options or you're already enrolled, understanding how to pay for college is one of the most important things you can do to set yourself up for success. The cost of college can seem overwhelming, but there are plenty of ways to make it more manageable.

In this chapter, we'll break down the different ways to finance your education, including scholarships, grants, loans, and budgeting tips to keep you on track. Paying for college might feel daunting, but with the right approach, you can reduce the financial stress and focus on what truly matters: your education.

Understanding the Cost of College

The first step in paying for college is understanding **how much it actually costs**. College costs vary widely depending on the school, your living situation, and your location, but the main expenses to consider are:

1. **Tuition**: This is the cost of the classes you take. It can vary depending on whether you go to a public or private school and whether you're an in-state or out-of-state student.
2. **Room and Board**: This includes housing and meals. Whether you live on-campus or off-campus, this is a significant part of your college expenses.

3. **Books and Supplies**: College textbooks are notoriously expensive. In addition to books, you'll need supplies like a laptop, notebooks, and other materials for your classes.

4. **Personal and Miscellaneous Expenses**: Things like transportation, laundry, and going out with friends can add up quickly, so it's important to budget for them as well.

Example:

Let's say you're attending a state school in your home state. The total cost might look something like this:

- **Tuition**: $10,000 per year
- **Room and Board**: $8,000 per year
- **Books and Supplies**: $1,200 per year
- **Personal Expenses**: $1,000 per year

This brings your total yearly cost to about **$20,200**—and that's before any financial aid.

Scholarships and Grants: Free Money!

Scholarships and grants are the **best kind of financial aid** because you don't have to pay them back. They're essentially **free money** that helps reduce your overall college costs. There are many opportunities to find scholarships and grants, and applying for them can make a huge difference in your college budget.

Scholarships:

Scholarships are typically awarded based on merit (like academic performance, athletic ability, or artistic talent) or specific criteria (like being from a certain region or demographic). There are **thousands** of scholarships out there, so it's important to apply to as many as possible. Here's how to get started:

- **Research**: Use websites like Schooly, Scholarships.com or Fastweb to find scholarships that match your qualifications.
- **Apply Early and Often**: Start looking for scholarships during your senior year of high school (or earlier) and keep applying throughout your college career. The more you apply, the better your chances.
- **Be Strategic**: Some scholarships are very specific (e.g., for students who love cats or who are pursuing a specific major), so be sure to read the requirements carefully and apply to ones that match your strengths.

Grants:

Grants are typically need-based and are often provided by the government or private organizations. One of the most common grants is the **Pell Grant**, which is available to students with significant financial need.

- **FAFSA**: To qualify for most federal grants and some state grants, you'll need to fill out the **Free Application for Federal Student Aid (FAFSA)**. This form determines your financial need and helps schools decide what type of financial aid you're eligible for.
- **State Grants**: Some states offer additional grants for residents, so check with your state's higher education department to see what's available.

Student Loans: Borrowing for College

While scholarships and grants are great, most students need to borrow money to cover the remaining cost of their education. That's where **student loans** come in.

There are two main types of student loans:

Federal Student Loans

Federal loans are often the best option because they usually have lower interest rates and more flexible repayment options.

- **Direct Subsidized Loans**: These loans are for students with financial need. The government pays the interest while you're in school at least half-time, so you don't have to worry about accruing interest right away.
- **Direct Unsubsidized Loans**: These loans are available to all students, regardless of need. However, interest starts accruing as soon as you take out the loan, so you'll owe more when you graduate.
- **PLUS Loans**: These loans are for parents of dependent students or for graduate/professional students. They typically have higher interest rates and require a credit check.

Tip: Always maximize your federal loans before considering private loans. Federal loans come with protections (like income-driven repayment plans) that private loans don't offer.

Private Student Loans

Private loans come from banks or other financial institutions and often have higher interest rates and less favorable repayment terms than federal loans. If you decide to take out a private loan, shop around for the best rates and repayment options.

How to Create a Budget for College

A **budget** is essential for managing your money in college. It will help you understand how much you can spend, save, and borrow, and it will keep you on track throughout the school year.

How to Set Up Your Budget:

1. **Track Your Income**: This includes any scholarships, grants, student loans, and part-time jobs. Be realistic about how much you can expect to earn.
2. **Estimate Your Expenses**: Break down your college expenses into categories, such as tuition, housing, food, books, transportation, and personal expenses.
3. **Subtract Your Expenses from Your Income**: This will help you see if you have any leftover funds or if you need to cut back on spending.
4. **Save for Emergencies**: Try to set aside some money for emergencies, even if it's just a small amount each month.

Tip: Use a budgeting app like **Mint** or **You Need a Budget (YNAB)** to track your income and expenses in real time.

Real-Life Examples: Paying for College

Sarah's Scholarship Success

Sarah is a high school senior who's been accepted to a state university. The total cost of her education (tuition, room, board, and books) comes to $25,000 per year. Initially, she was overwhelmed by the price tag, but she decided to apply for as many scholarships as possible.

After spending a few weeks researching scholarships, Sarah applied to 15 different opportunities. She received two scholarships: a **$5,000 merit-based scholarship** for her academic achievements and a **$2,000 community service scholarship** for her volunteer work with local organizations.

- **Total Scholarship Money**: $7,000
- **Remaining Balance**: $25,000 (total cost) - $7,000 (scholarships) = **$18,000**

Now, Sarah is able to cover a large portion of her tuition with scholarships, and she only needs to borrow $18,000 through federal student loans to finish her degree. By applying for multiple scholarships, Sarah reduced the amount she needed to borrow, which will save her money in the long run.

Mike's Budgeting Breakdown

Mike is a freshman at college and lives in a dorm on campus. He's been given a **$10,000 loan** to cover tuition, but he knows he needs to be smart with how he spends his money. Here's how he set up his budget for the semester:

- **Income**:
  - **Student Loan**: $10,000
  - **Part-time Job**: $2,500 (for the semester)
- **Expenses**:
  - **Tuition**: $6,000 (covered by the loan)
  - **Room and Board**: $3,000 (covered by the loan)
  - **Books**: $500
  - **Transportation**: $200 (bus pass for the semester)
  - **Personal Expenses** (eating out, shopping, etc.): $800

Mike's total expenses come to $10,500, but he's only borrowing $10,000 from his loan. That means he'll need to come up with an extra **$500** to cover everything.

Mike decides to reduce his personal expenses by cutting back on eating out and limiting his shopping. By carefully sticking to his budget, Mike avoids borrowing more money and stays on track to finish the semester without debt.

Emily's Loan Strategy

Emily has been accepted to a private university, and the total cost for the year is **$40,000**. She knows she'll have to borrow money to cover this cost, so she takes a careful approach to how she handles student loans.

Emily qualifies for both **federal loans** and a **private loan**. Here's how she breaks it down:

- **Federal Loans**: Emily is offered **$5,500 in Direct Subsidized Loans**, which have a lower interest rate and no interest accrues while she's in school.
- **Private Loan**: To cover the rest, Emily applies for a **private loan** for **$15,000**. The interest rate is higher, and interest begins accumulating immediately.

While it's tempting to borrow more through the private loan, Emily decides to take the lowest amount possible through the federal loans first. She also plans to work part-time while in school to help pay for books, transportation, and living expenses, which will reduce the amount of money she needs to borrow.

- **Federal Loan**: $5,500 (lower interest, subsidized)
- **Private Loan**: $15,000 (higher interest, accrues immediately)

By being strategic and borrowing the federal loans first, Emily saves money on interest in the long run and sets herself up to graduate with a manageable amount of debt.

Jessica's Financial Aid Package

Jessica is attending a private college that costs **$30,000** per year. She receives the following financial aid package:

- **Pell Grant**: $4,000 (federal grant for low-income students)
- **State Grant**: $2,000 (state-sponsored grant)
- **Merit Scholarship**: $5,000 (for her academic achievements)
- **Federal Student Loan**: $3,500 (Direct Subsidized Loan)
- **Remaining Balance**: $30,000 - $4,000 (Pell Grant) - $2,000 (State Grant) - $5,000 (Scholarship) - $3,500 (Loan) = **$15,500**

Jessica is still left with a balance of **$15,500**, but thanks to her grants and scholarships, she doesn't have to borrow as much through loans. Her remaining balance will be covered by a combination of **federal loans** and a **private loan** for the rest. With her grants, scholarships, and the federal loan, Jessica is in a much better position than if she had relied solely on loans.

Alternatives to Traditional College: Exploring Your Options

While college can be a great way to kickstart your career, it's not the only path to success. In fact, there are plenty of **alternative routes** that can help you achieve your goals without the weight of a massive student loan. Whether you're not sure if college is right for you, or you're looking for ways to avoid the high cost of tuition, there are options that may fit better with your needs, interests, and budget. Let's take a look at some of the most popular alternatives to traditional college:

Community College: A More Affordable Option

Community colleges offer a great way to get a higher education without the hefty price tag. The average cost of tuition at a community college is a fraction of what you'd pay at a four-year university. Plus, you can earn an associate degree or certificate that can help you enter the workforce, or you can transfer to a four-year university later if you choose.

- **Cost-Effective**: Community college tuition is significantly lower than that of most four-year schools, making it a more affordable way to complete general education courses or get specific training.
- **Flexibility**: Many community colleges offer evening and online courses, making it easier to balance work, family, and school.
- **Transfer Opportunities**: If you decide to pursue a bachelor's degree later on, many community colleges have transfer agreements with four-year universities, allowing you to continue your education at a lower cost.

Example:

Mark chose to attend a community college for two years to complete his general education requirements. He paid around $5,000 per year for tuition, which is far less than the $20,000 per year he would have spent at a four-year school. After graduating with an associate degree, he transferred to a state university and finished his bachelor's degree, saving a ton of money in the process.

Trade Schools and Apprenticeships: Hands-On Learning

If you're interested in a career that's more hands-on or in a specific trade, trade schools and apprenticeships are fantastic alternatives to traditional college. These programs are focused on practical skills that can help you land a job in industries like healthcare, construction, technology, and more.

- **Job-Specific Skills**: Trade schools provide the training you need for specific jobs, whether it's becoming a plumber, electrician, medical technician, or mechanic.
- **Shorter Programs**: Many trade school programs can be completed in less time than a four-year college degree, meaning you can start working and earning money faster.
- **High Earning Potential**: Many skilled trades offer competitive salaries, and in some fields, there's a shortage of workers, which can make your skills even more valuable.

Example:

Olivia enrolled in a 12-month medical assistant program at a trade school. By the time she finished, she had secured a full-time job at a doctor's office earning $40,000 a year—more than many of her friends with bachelor's degrees. Her program cost $10,000, and she was able to start working almost immediately, avoiding the need for student loans.

Online Courses and Certifications: Learn at Your Own Pace

Online learning platforms have exploded in popularity, offering affordable and flexible options for anyone who wants to gain new skills or certifications. Websites like **Coursera, Udemy**, and **LinkedIn Learning** provide access to a variety of courses in everything from coding to marketing, graphic design, and beyond.

- **Affordability**: Online courses can be much cheaper than traditional college tuition, with many options available for a fraction of the price.
- **Flexibility**: You can take courses at your own pace, so you can work around your schedule and learn on your own time.
- **Certifications**: Some online platforms offer certifications that are recognized by employers, which can help you gain a competitive edge in your job search.

Example:

Ethan wanted to break into digital marketing, but a traditional college degree wasn't in his plans. Instead, he completed a **Google Analytics certification** and a **SEO course** through **Coursera**, spending just a few hundred dollars. Within six months, he landed a marketing position at a tech company, where his new skills were more valuable than a degree would have been.

Starting Your Own Business: Entrepreneurship is an Option

If you have a passion for something and an entrepreneurial spirit, starting your own business might be the right path for you. You don't need a degree to start a business—what you need is determination, creativity, and a willingness to learn. Plus, there are plenty of resources available to help you get started.

- **Cost-Effective**: Starting a business can be much cheaper than attending college, especially if you're starting small (like an online shop, freelance service, or consulting business).
- **Flexibility and Independence**: Being your own boss means you control your schedule, your clients, and your earnings.

- **Learning by Doing**: As an entrepreneur, you'll learn valuable skills that go beyond what you'd learn in a classroom—skills like problem-solving, budgeting, and marketing.

Example:

Samantha always loved baking, so she decided to start a small cupcake business from home. With a $500 investment in equipment and ingredients, she started selling cupcakes at local farmers' markets and online. Within a year, her business was thriving, and she was earning more than many of her friends with college degrees.

Making the Right Choice for You

There's no one-size-fits-all answer when it comes to higher education. The traditional college route works for some, but it's not the best fit for everyone. The important thing is to choose the path that aligns with your goals, interests, and financial situation.

- **Think about your career goals**: Do you want a job that requires a specific degree? Or are you more interested in gaining practical, hands-on experience?
- **Consider the cost**: How much are you willing to spend on your education, and what will your return on investment be in terms of salary and career opportunities?
- **Take your time**: If you're unsure, consider taking a gap year to explore different options. You can use the time to work, travel, or pursue a hobby that could turn into a career.

No matter which route you choose, remember that education is about learning and growing. Whether it's through a traditional college degree, a trade school, or an entrepreneurial venture, what matters most is that you're investing in yourself.

Life lesson - a career should be something that brings you joy. If you just settle for a job because it pays the bills, you very well could end up miserable after a very short time. Do your due diligence and choose a career that makes you happy and reflects your personal values. There is nothing worse than accepting a job offer because you like the salary they offered you then find out two months in it is sucking the life out of you. Trust me on this.

Key Takeaways:
- **College is a major investment** in your future. It's important to understand the costs and explore funding options to minimize debt.
- **Start with the FAFSA**: Completing the Free Application for Federal Student Aid (FAFSA) is the first step in receiving financial aid, including grants, loans, and scholarships.
- **Explore scholarships and grants**: These are "free money" that doesn't need to be repaid. Apply for as many as possible to reduce tuition costs.
- **Understand student loans**: Federal loans often have lower interest rates and more flexible repayment options compared to private loans. Borrow wisely.
- **Consider alternatives**: Community colleges, trade schools, and online programs can offer a more affordable education, and many have transfer agreements with four-year universities.
- **Plan your college budget**: Consider tuition, room and board, textbooks, and other costs when planning. Use budgeting tools to track your expenses and make sure you can afford everything.

- **Consider a career plan**: Make sure your degree aligns with your career goals to avoid overspending on an education that won't help you achieve your aspirations.

Now that you have a clearer picture of how to finance your education, it's time to think about the bigger picture: your career. Your education is a stepping stone to your future career, and this chapter will help you navigate the process of **building a career** that aligns with your goals and passions. Whether you're just starting out or looking to grow professionally, we'll provide practical steps for setting career goals, finding job opportunities, and continuing your growth in the workforce.

Scholarship Tip:
Apply for as many scholarships as possible, even small ones! Every bit counts and adds up over time.

Student Loan Tip:
If you have federal student loans, explore income-driven repayment plans. These can adjust your payments based on what you earn, making your debt more manageable.

Chapter 7: Building Your Career

Launching and Growing Your Career: Key Steps for Success

"Choose a job you love, and you will never have to work a day in your life." ~ Confucius

Building a career isn't just about landing your first job; it's about finding meaningful work that aligns with your passions, goals, and lifestyle. Whether you're just starting out or looking to advance in your field, this chapter will give you the tools and strategies you need to build a successful career.

In this chapter, we'll talk about how to identify your career goals, find the right job opportunities, develop the skills you need to stand out, and take steps to grow professionally. A fulfilling career takes time to build, but with the right mindset and approach, you can create a path that not only provides financial stability but also gives you personal satisfaction.

Identifying Your Career Goals

Before you can build a career, you need to have a clear understanding of what you want to achieve. Career goals help you stay focused and motivated as you work your way up the ladder.

What Are Career Goals?

Career goals are the professional milestones you want to reach—whether it's a specific job title, skillset, salary, or industry. Setting goals helps you create a roadmap for your career and gives you something to work toward.

How to Set Your Career Goals:

1. **Start with Short-Term Goals**: These might include getting your first job, gaining a certain skill, or completing an internship. Short-term goals should be achievable in the next 6 months to 1 year.

2. **Long-Term Goals**: Think about where you want to be in 5, 10, or even 20 years. Do you see yourself in a leadership role? Do you want to start your own business? Your long-term goals will guide your decisions in the short term.

3. **Break It Down**: Once you've set your big goals, break them into smaller, actionable steps. For example, if your goal is to be a marketing manager in 5 years, a smaller goal might be to complete a certification in digital marketing within the next 6 months.

Finding the Right Job Opportunities

With your career goals in mind, the next step is to start looking for job opportunities that align with those goals. Whether you're starting from scratch or looking for a new position, knowing where to look and how to apply is key.

Where to Look for Jobs:

1. **Job Boards and Websites**: Websites like **LinkedIn**, **Indeed**, **Glassdoor**, and **CareerBuilder** are excellent places to search for open positions. Make sure to update your resume and LinkedIn profile regularly so you can apply quickly when opportunities arise.

2. **Networking**: Building relationships with people in your industry is one of the most effective ways to find job opportunities. Attend

industry events, participate in online forums, and connect with people on LinkedIn.

3. **Internships and Entry-Level Jobs**: If you're just starting out, internships and entry-level jobs can provide valuable experience. Even if a position isn't your dream job, it can open doors to future opportunities.

How to Apply:

- **Tailor Your Resume**: Customize your resume for each job application by highlighting the skills and experience that are most relevant to the position.

- **Write a Strong Cover Letter**: Your cover letter is your chance to show your enthusiasm and explain why you're a great fit for the job. Be sure to make it personalized and specific to the company.

- **Prepare for Interviews**: Research the company and the role, practice common interview questions, and be ready to discuss how your skills and experience make you a good fit for the position.

Building Skills to Stand Out

In today's competitive job market, it's essential to develop skills that will help you stand out from the crowd. Employers look for candidates who have both technical and soft skills.

Technical Skills

Technical skills are job-specific abilities that you can learn through formal education, on-the-job training, or self-study. Examples include programming, graphic design, data analysis, and project management.

Soft Skills

Soft skills are personal attributes that help you interact effectively with others. These include communication, problem-solving, time management, and teamwork. Soft skills are important in every job and can make the difference between a good employee and a great one.

How to Build Your Skills:

- **Take Online Courses**: Websites like **Coursera**, **Udemy**, and **Skillshare** offer affordable courses that can help you learn new skills or enhance the ones you already have.
- **Seek Out Mentors**: A mentor can provide guidance, feedback, and advice based on their experience in the industry. Don't be afraid to ask someone you respect for mentorship.
- **Practice and Apply**: The best way to improve your skills is through practice. Look for opportunities to apply what you're learning in real-world scenarios, whether that's through a side project, volunteer work, or freelancing.

Growing Your Career: Networking and Professional Development

Building your career doesn't stop once you land your first job. To advance and grow, you'll need to continually invest in your professional development and expand your network.

Networking: The Key to Career Growth

Networking is one of the most effective ways to open doors to new opportunities. By building relationships with professionals in your field, you can learn about job openings, get career advice, and receive referrals.

- **Attend Industry Events**: Conferences, meetups, and webinars are great opportunities to meet people in your field.

- **Join Professional Organizations**: Many industries have professional groups or associations that offer networking opportunities, resources, and support for career development.
- **Stay Active on LinkedIn**: LinkedIn is a powerful tool for networking. Connect with colleagues, join groups related to your industry, and share articles or insights to stay visible.

Professional Development: Keep Learning

The world of work is constantly changing, so it's important to keep learning and growing in your field.

- **Pursue Advanced Certifications or Degrees**: If you're in a field where additional certifications or education are required for advancement (like project management or IT), consider investing in them.
- **Seek Out Feedback**: Regularly ask for feedback from managers and colleagues to identify areas for improvement and set new goals for yourself.

Self-Assessments: Understanding Your Strengths and Career Fit

Before diving into your career journey, it's helpful to get a better understanding of yourself—your skills, interests, and values. Self-assessments can provide valuable insights into your strengths and help you identify career paths that align with who you are. Whether you're deciding on a major, switching careers, or just looking for direction, these assessments can help clarify your next steps.

There are several online tools available to guide you through this process:

- **MyNextMove**: This tool helps you explore career options based on your interests, skills, and experience. Take their interactive assessment to discover potential career paths.

- **CareerOneStop**: Sponsored by the U.S. Department of Labor, this site offers a variety of assessments, including career exploration and skills assessments, to help you make informed decisions about your future.
- **The Myers-Briggs Type Indicator (MBTI)**: Understanding your personality type can give you deeper insights into the kinds of work environments and roles that will suit you best. Various free versions of the MBTI test are available online to get started.

By using these self-assessments, you can gain clarity about where your passions and skills align, allowing you to make more informed decisions as you pursue your career.

Finding the right career path is about discovering what makes you feel fulfilled and successful, both now and in the future. Take your time, explore, and remember that it's okay to adjust your course along the way.

Key Takeaways

- **Set clear career goals** to stay focused and motivated as you build your career.
- **Look for job opportunities** through job boards, networking, and internships.
- **Develop a mix of technical and soft skills** to stand out to employers.
- **Invest in your professional growth** by networking and continuing to learn new skills.
- **Networking** is essential for career growth—build relationships and connect with professionals in your field.

Next Steps

- **Set your career goals**: Write down your short-term and long-term career goals, and break them down into actionable steps.
- **Start networking**: Reach out to professionals in your field and attend industry events, either in person or online.
- **Develop your skills**: Take a course, volunteer, or look for side projects that help you build the skills you need to advance your career.
- **Look for job opportunities**: Start applying for internships or entry-level jobs, and customize your resume and cover letter for each position.

⚑ Career Tip:

Don't underestimate the value of networking. Many job opportunities come from relationships, not just job boards.

▨ Job Search Reminder:

Customize your resume and cover letter for each job you apply for. Tailoring your application shows the employer you've done your research and are truly interested in the position.

Internships: Gaining Experience and Building Connections

One of the best ways to start building your career early is by completing an **internship**. Internships provide invaluable hands-on experience, help you network with professionals in your field, and make you stand out to future employers.

Why Internships Matter

Internships allow you to gain experience in the field you're interested in. You'll learn new skills, get a feel for the work environment, and see if the career path you're considering is the right fit for you. Even if the internship doesn't lead to a full-time job right away, the experience will help you refine your resume and build a network of contacts that could help you later on.

How to Find an Internship

Many colleges have resources and partnerships with businesses to help students secure internships. Websites like **Internships.com**, **LinkedIn**, and **Handshake** are also great places to search for opportunities. When applying for internships, make sure your resume highlights relevant skills, even if they're from part-time jobs or volunteer work. Don't forget to write a compelling cover letter that shows your enthusiasm for the role.

The Benefits of Internships

- **Gain Real-World Experience**: Get a taste of what the job will really be like.
- **Build Your Resume**: Employers want to see that you've had relevant experience.

- **Make Connections**: Internships are a great way to meet industry professionals who can offer advice and help you with job leads in the future.

Money Mistakes to Avoid in Your 20s

"Your 20s are a time to build the foundation for your financial future—make sure you're building it on solid ground." ~ Suze Orman

---

The decisions you make in your 20s will shape your financial future. It's a time to establish good habits, learn from mistakes, and set yourself up for long-term success. But there are common money mistakes that many young adults make—and if you avoid them, you'll be miles ahead of the game.

Mistake #1: Living Beyond Your Means

It's easy to fall into the trap of **spending more than you make**, especially with credit cards and student loans. But carrying too much debt or relying on credit to fund a lifestyle you can't afford is a quick way to dig yourself into a financial hole.

- **Solution**: Create a budget that aligns with your income and stick to it. If you don't have enough money for something, don't buy it—save for it instead.

Mistake #2: Ignoring Your Credit Score

Your credit score can affect many aspects of your life—from renting an apartment to getting a car loan or mortgage. But many young adults don't realize how important their credit is until it's too late.

- **Solution**: Start building credit early by getting a credit card and paying it off each month. Always monitor your credit report and make sure there are no errors that could negatively affect your score.

Mistake #3: Not Saving for Emergencies

Life happens—cars break down, medical bills pile up, and unexpected expenses always seem to arise. Without an **emergency fund**, these situations can lead to debt or financial stress.

- **Solution**: Build an emergency fund of at least 3 to 6 months' worth of living expenses. Keep it in a separate savings account, so you don't dip into it for regular purchases.

Mistake #4: Avoiding Investing

Many young adults wait to invest, thinking they need to have a lot of money saved up first. The truth is, the earlier you start, the more time your money has to grow.

- **Solution**: Start small by investing in a retirement account, like a 401(k) or an IRA, and take advantage of employer match programs. Even small contributions now can lead to big rewards later.

Mistake #5: Not Planning for the Future

It's easy to get caught up in the present and forget about the future. But whether it's saving for retirement, buying a house, or paying off debt, planning ahead is crucial for long-term financial success.

- **Solution**: Set financial goals for the next 5, 10, and 20 years. Break them down into manageable steps, and create a plan to work toward them.

By avoiding these common mistakes, you'll be setting yourself up for financial stability and growth. Your 20s are the perfect time to learn, plan, and start building a solid financial foundation for your future.

Wrapping Up Finance 101

Congratulations on completing *Finance 101*! By working through this guide, you've taken a big step toward building a solid financial foundation. From understanding income basics and budgeting to managing debt and saving for the future, you've gained valuable knowledge that will serve you well as you navigate adulthood. Remember, personal finance is a journey, and the skills you've learned here will continue to grow with you as you make financial decisions.

This is just the beginning! Keep an eye out for more additions to the *Adulting Made Simplish* series. Upcoming guides will explore other essential life skills, giving you practical, straightforward advice for handling the challenges that come with growing independence. Each book in the series is designed to empower you, simplify complex topics, and help you feel more confident in your journey to adulthood.

Thank you for joining us on this journey—and happy adulting!

BONUS TRACKERS

Financial Goal

START DATE _____ DEADLINE: _____

FINANCIAL GOAL: _____

THE PLAN

_____
_____

THE PLAN

_____
_____
_____

MOTIVATION

_____
_____
_____
_____
_____

HABITS I'D LIKE TO CONTINUE

_____
_____
_____
_____

HABITS I NEED TO BREAK

_____
_____
_____
_____

ACTION STEPS	DUE DATE

THINGS THAT WENT WELL

_____
_____

WHAT DON'T GO SO WELL?

_____
_____

LESSONS I HAVE LEARNED

_____
_____

COMPLETION DATE:

Budget
Overview

No.	Income	Amount	Total Debt

No.	Expenses	Amount	Total Debt

Total Savings :

Budget Planner

Month of

Income Streams

After Tax	Budget	Actual	Differences
Income			
Side Hustles			
Business			
Others			

Fixed & Variable Expenses

Expenses	Budget	Actual	Differences

Total Income (After Tax)

Total Fixed Expenses

Total Variable Expenses

Savings - Income + Expenses

Monthly Budget

GOAL

EXPENSES

INCOME -1

MONTH

INCOME -2

OTHER INCOME

BUDGET

Total Income

Bill to Be Paid	Due Date	Amount	Paid

Monthly Summary

Total Income	Total Expenses	Difference

Notes

Credit Score Tracker

TOP FINANCIAL GOAL :   DATE :

CURRENT SCORE :   GOAL SCORE:

—

—

—

—

—

—

—

—

—

—

JAN | FEB | MAR | APR | MAY | JUN | JUL | AUG | SEP | OCT | NOV | DEC

NOTES

Credit Score
Improvement

CURRENT CREDIT SCORE

CREDIT SCORE GOAL

TOP THREE PRIORITIES

1	2	3

ACTION STEPS	IMPACT ON SCORE

NOTES

Upcoming Expenses

YEAR:

January	February	March

April	May	June

July	August	September

October	November	December

Weekly Expenses

Description	Amount	Date :
Monday		Note :
Tuesday		
Wednesday		
Thursday		
Friday		Weekly goals :
		1.
		2.
		3.
Saturday		4.
		5.
		6.
		7.
Sunday		

Expenses Log

Date	Category	Description	Methods	Amount

Spending Tracker

Date	Description	Category	Amount
		Total	

Utility Bills Tracker

☆ ELECTRONICS

MONTH	AMOUNT	MONTH	AMOUNT
JANURARY		JULY	
FEBRURY		AUGUST	
MARCH		SEPTEMBER	
APRIL		OCTOBER	
MAY		NOVEMBER	
JUNE		DECEMBER	

☆ WATER

MONTH	AMOUNT	MONTH	AMOUNT
JANURARY		JULY	
FEBRURY		AUGUST	
MARCH		SEPTEMBER	
APRIL		OCTOBER	
MAY		NOVEMBER	
JUNE		DECEMBER	

☆ GAS

MONTH	AMOUNT	MONTH	AMOUNT
JANURARY		JULY	
FEBRURY		AUGUST	
MARCH		SEPTEMBER	
APRIL		OCTOBER	
MAY		NOVEMBER	
JUNE		DECEMBER	

Subscription Tracker

Month:

Date	Bill	Amount	Frequency		Auto Renew
			Monthly	Yearly	

Debt Payment Tracker

Min. Payment :   Total Payment :

Paid	Balance	Paid	Balance

Savings Overview

Savings Goals

Actual Savings

What motivates me to save money?

How can I stay motivated?

Saving Goals

Saving For : _____

Amount : _____

Target Date : _____

Summary

Week Month	Goal	Actual	Remaining	Notes
Total :				

Check us out at

www.adultingmadesimplish.com

for free downloads of budget, expense, savings trackers, and more!

Made in the USA
Las Vegas, NV
10 February 2025

17858920R00066